DIGGING
AND
DELIGHTED

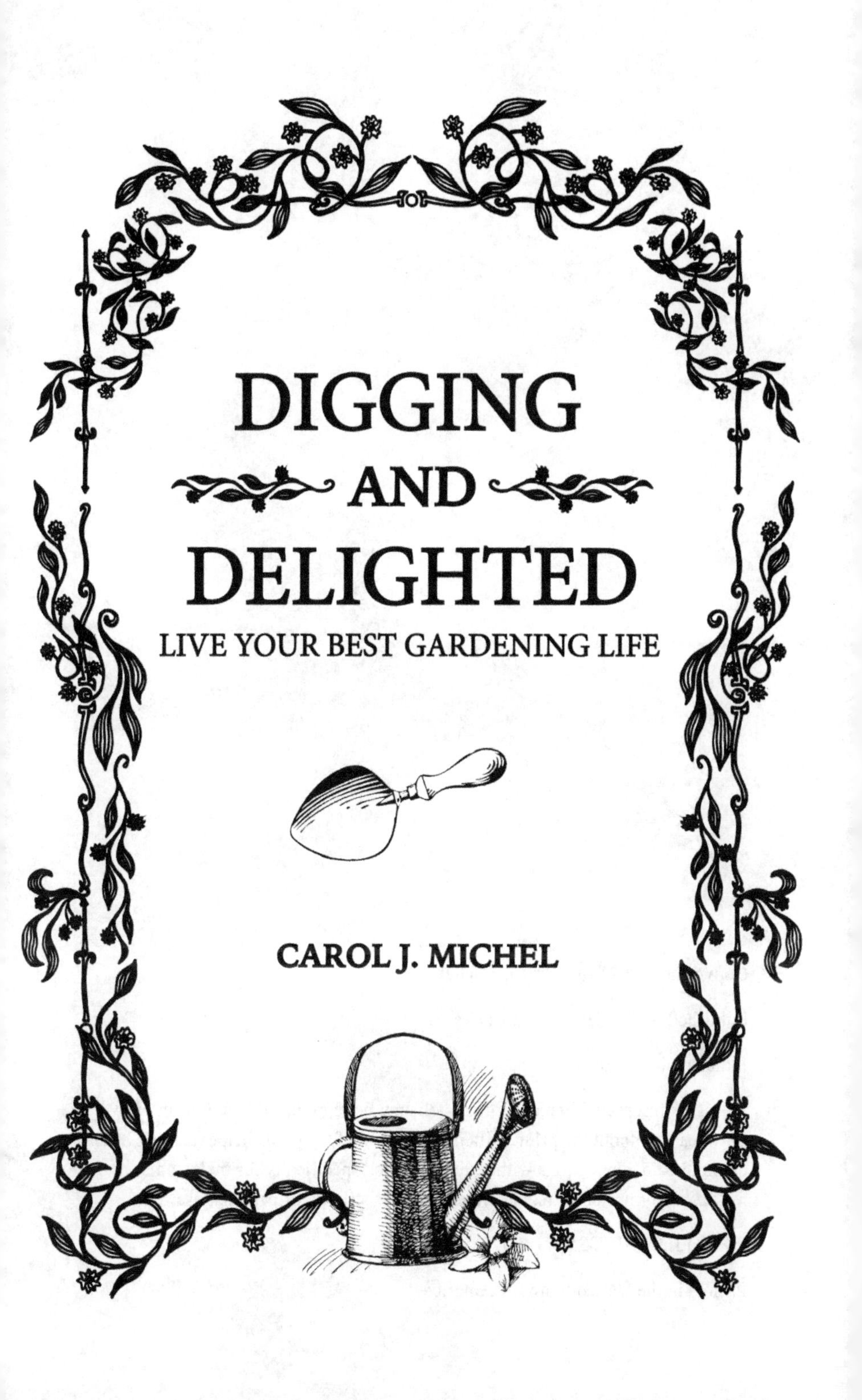

DIGGING AND DELIGHTED

LIVE YOUR BEST GARDENING LIFE

CAROL J. MICHEL

Published by Gardenangelist Books

Indianapolis, Indiana

ISBN-13: 978-1-7335009-7-5

Printed in the United States of America

For all who garden

CONTENTS

I
HELLO

Hello, and welcome to the world of gardening!

This is the book that's going to change your gardening life and make it better than you ever imagined. It's going to do it with a combination of humor and good advice, and it will be applicable wherever you happen to put down roots.

I want you to know, from the start, that I wrote this book so you would have a guide to help you think like a gardener and feel confident as you step out into your garden, whether that garden is just one houseplant in a four-inch clay pot or a huge garden covering several acres out in the country.

I also want you to know, up front, that this book is different from almost every other gardening book you've ever read.

The first difference is that this book is small enough that you could carry it in a bag or put it in a big pocket. I want you to carry this book around with you so you can pull it out to read instead of grabbing your smartphone to scroll through screen after screen of nothing in particular, but you scroll anyway because it's something to do. Now your something to do will be to read this book. I also want you to be able to read this book in bed or while sitting out in a garden or on the steps of your porch as you look out at what will one day be your dream garden.

I want you to underline passages that speak to you, put an asterisk next to paragraphs that you want to re-read, and make notes in the margins. I want you to dog-ear the corners when a page strikes your fancy. I want to see smudges of dirt on the pages or maybe a pretty leaf stuck in a random page because you read this book outdoors in your garden and the leaf just seemed too pretty not to keep.

Second, there are no pictures. No glossy, drool-worthy photos of gardens. Wait a minute! Doesn't every book about gardening have pictures in it? Perhaps you think I've broken a fundamental rule of gardening books. I assure you, I haven't broken any rules. And if I have, it's for your benefit.

There are no pictures because I don't want you to think about a particular garden or flower or tree that I've chosen for you to see. I want you to picture *your* garden when you read this book. If you are looking for pictures, go to the Internet where there are millions of pictures of gardens in every conceivable climate. Or take pictures of your own garden and stick them in this book wherever you'd like to see a picture. I want you to imagine your idea of a garden when you read this book.

Where are the lists of plants? You guessed correctly if you realized without even reading every word of this book (which you will surely—hopefully—do soon enough) that there will be no lists of plants. No list of best shrubs for shady gardens, no top ten cacti to grow in a desert garden, no five houseplants you can't live without for a minute longer. No particular flower, tree, shrub, or vegetable is endorsed, though there might be a few mentions for purposes of illustration. (Wait, I said no pictures, so make that for purposes of explanation.) Please don't think I'm putting down gardening books with pictures or lists. There is a place for them in your library of gardening, as there is a place for a book like this one.

Now, let's talk for a minute about you. How did you get to this world of gardening? Are you the last person people thought would care about flowers in your front garden or where your tomatoes came from, but now you find yourself doing research to figure out which of this year's new varieties of tomatoes you should plant in your vegetable garden? Are you now thinking you really must learn more about *Clematis* and the proper way to pronounce it, because someone casually suggested you have the perfect spot for one?

Maybe a friend asked you to stop by and water their houseplants while they were away, assuring you it wasn't hard to do at all, and you found yourself lingering in their living room because it was so welcoming with all the plants. Then you decided to get a houseplant or two for your own living room, and that turned out to be a slippery slope that led to more houseplants than you ever intended to own.

Yet, you are still reluctant to call yourself a gardener. The plants in your garden are growing, more or less, but you still feel like a fake. When you're around other gardeners, the ones you consider real gardeners, you think you don't really know that much about gardening in general. Will you ever know enough to walk with that certain swagger that shows you mean business in the garden center to look over the hostas to find the perfect one? Plus, you aren't old. Aren't gardeners old people who have nothing better to do than fuss over their roses or fret about when the pansies are going to go on sale in the spring?

Perhaps you've considered yourself a gardener for some time but feel like you could use a little boost to your morale because there is that one houseplant everyone else grows that always dies in your care. For the life of you, you don't know why. Or maybe a storm knocked out the tree that provided your garden with shade, and now you must relearn how to grow plants in full sun. Or you just feel like your garden hasn't reached its true potential, and you'd like to up your gardening game.

You may be wondering how all this is going to happen. Who is going to show you the way to becoming a better gardener or convince you that you're already a good, perhaps great, gardener?

Well, you've just taken a big first step forward to becoming a great or greater gardener because you're holding this book and have read this far. It's fate! This is the moment you'll look back on and say, "That's when my garden and I really started to connect."

Whether your knowledge level is, "Wait, those green things are plants?" or you not only know those green things are plants but also what family, genus, and species they belong to, reading this book is just what you need right now.

Of course, I would love to actually be there with you, wherever you are, to act as your guide, giving you encouragement and answering each and every one of your gardening questions as they pop into your head. (Forgive me for that one tiny little lie. I really wouldn't like to answer each and every gardening question that pops into your head. I'd like you to think and do a little research on your own first. You'll learn more that way and won't rely on me as the heroine who holds up your gardening world.)

I'd love to be sitting behind a big tree at the edge of your garden, ready to step out and pick you up when you trip over that proverbial rake. Or maybe pop up above a hedge and tell you it will be okay when you awkwardly prune your roses or spill a packet of tiny seeds.

I'll be like Yoda when he was providing guidance for Luke Skywalker as he became a Jedi knight. Teach you to become a gardener, I will.

Just think of me as your eccentric gardening aunt, that one whose neighbors think she's a little crazy because, well, just look at her garden! I'm here to guide you as you become a great gardener, living your best gardening life.

Shall we get started?

2

WEATHER THE WEATHER

The weather takes on more importance when you garden.

Do you remember the drought of 2012 that caused gardeners across the United States to consider collecting their tears as a means of watering their gardens? There was also some wailing and gnashing of teeth when many were told they could no longer run sprinklers or irrigation systems because reservoirs and wells were drained to unimagined low levels. In a few places, old towns that were sacrificed decades earlier to form reservoirs resurfaced as water levels dropped.

We were reminded that water is a finite resource. For much of that summer, we were allowed to water only newly planted trees and shrubs and vegetable gardens as long as we were standing there holding the hose and not using the forbidden sprinkler.

Another memory from that summer occurred when my then 24-year-old nephew casually mentioned he'd heard it had been a dry summer. He heard? A dry summer? Didn't he notice it for himself? Didn't he read the newspapers or watch the news?

Perhaps not. He didn't have his own yard or a garden to fret over. His life went on, uninterrupted, by the worst drought of my gardening life.

Now that you are a gardener, weather takes on more importance. Depending on where you're gardening, you want to know several things about your weather besides how much rain to expect. Once you know these things, you can choose plants accordingly or make plans to water when needed.

You need to know when to expect frost in your garden, especially the last frost of the spring and the first frost of the fall. Your growing season lies between these two dates. Those dates dictate when you can plant tender plants like tomatoes outside with a reasonable assurance that you won't have to cover them or, worse yet, dig them up and bring them back inside when a late spring frost threatens.

In some years, you'll face a late soul-crushing garden frost, no matter how watchful you are. And the first time it happens to you, nipping your early planting plans in the bud, you'll lose some plants. Even experienced gardeners occasionally look at extended forecasts, decide that frost is in the rear-view mirror, and then get caught by a late dip in temperatures.

By the way, that first frost at the end of the growing season? Many gardeners are happy to see it arrive, to call an end to the growing season so they can clean up the garden, put their tools away, and rest for a few months. I'm one of those gardeners! Believe it or not, I enjoy thinking about other things through winter when the garden is on its own. Things like what I'm going to plant in the garden the next spring. Which isn't the same as thinking about what I have to do in the garden during the growing season. Trust me on this.

If you garden where there is no frost, then you have the opportunity to garden outside year-round. Congratulations, no rest for you! Those of us with changing seasons enjoy the time between the first fall frost and the last spring frost to rest a bit, plan next year's garden, travel without having to round up someone to water the plants, mow the lawn, harvest produce, etc. while we're gone.

Finally, you should learn how cold it gets in your garden in the wintertime and how long it stays cold. Those two pieces of information put your garden into a hardiness zone. Be aware that official maps in some older gardening books showing hardiness zones across the United States and Canada may be out of date. Today, you can easily find the most current USDA hardiness zone map online, pinpoint where you live and garden, and determine your hardiness zone. Remember your zone! Then, when you look at a plant's descriptions, you can check its hardiness zone range and determine right away if it will survive winters in your garden.

With your new weather knowledge and awareness, you are almost ready to start gardening.

3

FIND WINDOWS OF OPPORTUNITY

Learn the calendar for your climate, and plan your garden activities accordingly.

As soon as we have a few warm early spring days, new gardeners start singing: "Is it too early? Is it too early?" Then, one day, when it's as hot as summer, they change their chorus to: "Is it too late? Is it too late?"

To live your best gardening life, you should figure out when is the best time to do what needs to be done in your garden.

But don't get too uptight and look for the perfect time for everything you do in a garden. Timing in the garden isn't as precise as some gardeners think it is. There are simply too many variables, primarily the weather. (Which is consistently a variable, so does that make it a constant?)

Some years, mid-March, around St. Patrick's Day, might be the perfect time for me to sow seeds for peas. Then another year we might have an earlier than normal spring, and early March is a good time to sow peas. Worst case, we have a horrible winter and the ground doesn't warm up enough to sow peas until late

March or early April. Maybe you've figured out that mid-March is the perfect time to sow peas in your area, too, but you were busy that week or on vacation and didn't get it done. Does that mean it's too late to sow peas in late March?

Nope. Most of the time, gardeners work with windows of opportunity, not precision timing. A few warm days at the end of February in my garden is a window of opportunity to do some pruning on trees and shrubs, which are best pruned in early spring when temperatures are above freezing. But it's not a good window of opportunity to prune spring flowering shrubs like lilacs and forsythia which set their flower buds in the fall. If you trim them in early spring, you'll remove the flowers you've waited all winter to see.

There are windows of opportunity for just about anything you want or need to do in a garden. The trick is to recognize them and then take advantage of them. Sometimes, opening those windows of opportunity is something gardeners learn to do by watching that crazy gardening lady in the neighborhood, the one who is always the first to plant pansies in the spring. The one who is still shoving bulbs into the ground in November. The one who can be seen with loads of produce picked from her garden in mid-summer. She probably has this whole timing thing figured out and would gladly explain it to you. Or, if there is no crazy gardening lady near you, you can also check with your Cooperative Extension service. Most of them publish calendars online to show when to do what in your area.

Because here's the other thing about timing. It's local. What is just in time in my Midwestern garden might be too late in a southern garden or way too early in a northern garden or make no sense at all in a Florida garden. And all bets are off in California. So, find that nearby gardener, find your local information, and synchronize your calendar. You don't want to miss out on your own window of opportunity for living your best gardening life.

4
LEARN ABOUT YOUR SOIL

Your soil is the foundation of your garden, and upon its health rests the well-being of every plant. Nurture it first to ensure a healthy garden.

I WAS surprised one day when I was looking at my dad's high school yearbook to find out that he was on a soil judging team. I had never heard of a soil judging team, in spite of attending an agricultural college.

My main question was, what does a soil judging team do? How does one go about judging soils? Is there a talent competition? An award for most congenial soil? Do the judges interview the soil before crowning one of them Miss Soil? So many questions.

I was not even close to the truth about soil judging. Soil judging teams— yes, there are still soil judging teams today at both the high school and collegiate levels— judge soils and compete to determine who is the best soil judge. They eventually use their soil judging skills when they become crop and soil scientists, vital cogs in the engine that produces our food.

At this point, you might be wondering if learning to judge soils is required to be a gardener. No, it's not. But knowing what type of soil you have in your garden and, perhaps more importantly, how to improve that soil helps to shape your destiny as a gardener. Ask any gardener who struggles with heavy clay soils. Or a gardener who tries to grow food on a sandy beach. They both envy that gardener who has loamy, organically rich soil.

Would you like to try judging some soils? You've read this far, so I'm going to assume that yes, you do.

The most basic way to judge your soil is to rub some of it between your thumb and index finger. Can you form it into a lovely ribbon of soil? Yes? Oh, that is not good. That probably means your soil has a high clay content. Soils with high clay contents are used to make bricks. Bricks are a good choice for a well-built house or a solid path through your garden but aren't great for plants.

Does your soil feel all gritty and rough, like it might cut you into a million pieces? If yes, then your soil has a high sand content which means it's likely to dry out quickly. Your plants may always be thirsty and not at all happy, unless your garden is in a desert with desert-type plants.

If your soil sample is smooth and crumbly, then you have hit the gardening jackpot with a lovely, silty loam soil.

You can also learn about your soil by asking neighbors who garden about their soil, keeping in mind that theirs might be lovely because they added organic matter to it over the years or brought in top soil or otherwise amended their dirt to make it perfect gardening soil. Or look up your local Cooperative Extension Service website and read what they have written about soils in your area and where they recommend sending soil for further testing.

Further testing? It sure sounds like I'm making dirt complicated. Well, spend a few minutes talking to a pedologist about pedology—the study of soils—and my explanations here will sound like those of a simpleton. Further testing will give you a more detailed chemical analysis and let you know if your soil has a good amount of nitrogen, potassium, phosphorus, and other elements needed for plant growth. It will also tell you whether your soil pH is alkaline or acidic, which is good to know because some plants, like blueberries and azaleas, sulk if the soil pH isn't to their liking.

Plus, depending on where you live, some tests will tell you about heavy metals or other pollutants that may have contaminated your soil. But this isn't important unless you are planning to grow lots of vegetables. Oops. Now I've scared you. Relax. The likelihood that you are gardening on a toxic waste site is extremely low. Anyway, don't take notes on soil fertility just yet. We will get to all of that in a later chapter.

In the meantime, I think it's okay to start digging and planting without doing extensive soil judging and testing. You will probably be okay, unless you need a pickaxe to dig. In that case, check to see if you are digging on your patio.

If you are, move over into the garden. If that didn't help and the digging is still rough going, consider moving entirely to a new house and garden because using a pickaxe to dig in the garden isn't going to be much fun. If you can't move, your best gardening life probably involves container gardening. More on that soon.

5
LEARN A NEW LANGUAGE

Botanical Latin, a written—not spoken—universal language ensures you get the plant you want.

WOULD you like to plant a daisy in your garden? Daisies are lovely, cheery flowers, usually with a bright yellow center surrounded by white petals, although sometimes they have colored petals. Let's imagine that one day you decide a daisy is just what your garden needs! So, you go to the local garden center and ask them if they have any daisies for sale.

The first thing they will ask you is, "What kind of daisy are you looking for?"

At this point, telling them you are looking for the plant kind of daisy won't be helpful. If you tell them you want the white one with the yellow center, that will narrow down your choices a bit, but you still might not get what you were hoping for. Why? Because "daisy" is a common name, and a common name can apply to many different plants. Without batting an eye, I can come up with several daisies including Shasta daisies, ox-eye daisies, marguerite daisies, blue-eyed daisies, English daisies, African daisies, Gerbera daisies … I think you get the idea.

To get the exact plant we want, we gardeners who are trying to live our best gardening lives refer to plants by their botanical names. Of course, this assumes we know the botanical name of the plant we want, and the little secret is that we often don't. Or maybe we know the botanical name but we're afraid we'll mispronounce it and embarrass ourselves, so we won't say it out loud.

But here's the secret of the language known as botanical Latin. It isn't a spoken language. It's a written language. Of course, we still must say the words on occasion, such as when we are asking for a *Leucanthemum vulgare*, which is the ox-eye daisy, or *Leucanthemum* x *superbum*, which is the Shasta daisy.

How do we know how to pronounce anything in this written language if it isn't spoken? The truth is, we don't know for certain how to say many of these words, we just give it our best shot. Or we hear someone else say a botanical name—someone we think is a better, smarter gardener than we are—and we imitate how they say it. We can also go on to the Internet and do a search for "how to pronounce" followed by the plant name and come up with sites that will pronounce it for us.

My personal belief is that however you would like to pronounce a botanical name is fine. You may pronounce the last part of *Leucanthemum* x *superbum* as "Super Bum" or "Su Perbum." By the way, in my world, pronouncing the "x" is optional, though most pronunciation guides include it in the name.

Are your eyes glazing over at this marvelous world of botanical Latin? Before you get completely lost, I feel it's worth mentioning that all plants are put into plant families. Within the plant families, they are sometimes divided into subfamilies. Each plant ends up with its own genus and species which becomes its name. And it's the same name no matter where you find the plant and what spoken language they use in that location.

That is, until the plant taxonomists, who get to name all the plants, decide that a plant isn't what they thought it was, so they change its name to something else and then put out the word about the new name. Yes, these occasional name changes sometimes confound even those who have been gardening a long time.

Some gardeners continue to call plants by their old names out of habit or preference or because new names just don't catch on at the local garden centers. I still call my New England asters *Aster novae-angliae* because the new name of *Symphyotrichum novae-angliae* is not only nearly unpronounceable, it's also harder to spell. I have friends who just refer to them as "formerly known as aster."

One last bit of advice about botanical names and Latin and the reluctance of some new gardeners of saying these names out loud in front of other people: Be brave and use them. My own last name (flip to the cover to see if you've forgotten it already) appears to have several correct pronunciations based on its spelling. Michael? Michelle? Mitchell? Even within my own extended family, different branches have adopted different pronunciations. I assure you I have answered to all those pronunciations without being offended.

Likewise, I've never seen a plant curl up its leaves, droop its branches, or close up its flowers because of how someone said its botanical name in its presence. My advice is to ignore the intimidating aspects of this new language. Learn and embrace enough botanical Latin to ensure you get the daisy you want in your garden.

6

GROW PLANTS YOU LOVE

When you invest time and money in a garden, it's more fun if you love the plants.

SOME ADVICE just seems so obvious it's almost embarrassing to mention it. Advice like, "grow the plants you love." After all, you're soon going to find out, or perhaps already know, that gardening can involve some serious time and energy. And money.

Therefore, if you want to live your best gardening life, learn which plants you love. But I must warn you, figuring out which plants you love may involve growing a lot of plants and, over time, discarding the ones you discover you don't love.

One way to assess plants is to visit other gardens and see what strike your fancy. If you find yourself falling in love with a plant someone else is growing, ask them questions about it. See for yourself where it's growing and honestly ask if you can give it the same type of environment. After all, it's no use buying a perennial flower that likes shade if your garden is in full sun and vice versa, or trying to grow a plant that prefers a bog when your garden is in the middle of a desert.

I know from my vast, extensive personal experience that you are likely to love almost all plants when you see them potted up and pruned and on their best behavior at a garden center. Unfortunately, you have no idea if you will still love them when they grow to full size in your garden, or wilt in your sun, or grow spindly in your shade.

Of course, the upside of falling in love with a plant at a garden center is you know right away where you can find and purchase those plants for your garden. Right there it is in front of you for sale! Compare that to the downside of falling head over gardening boots for a plant in someone else's garden and finding out that it's next to impossible to find that one-of-a-kind plant that you're now madly in love with and that you feel you must now grow in your own garden, regardless of what it will cost you.

Since you are going to fall madly in love with plants while living your best gardening life, at least know what type of plant you are falling in love with… their parentage, their natural climate, their ways about the garden.

Annual flowers, usually bought in the spring, grown all summer, and then discarded in the fall because their life cycle ends in one season, are no big loss if you discover you don't love them like you thought you would. Your investment wasn't that great considering all the future seasons you plan to spend in your garden. You simply make note that you didn't like those annuals and buy different annuals the next spring. Good-bye, weird colored petunias that languished after mid-summer. Never again, persnickety plant with blue flowers that stopped blooming right after you potted it up.

Biennials—slow-growing plants that sit around the first year looking all leafy, go dormant for the winter, and then return the next spring to send up a flower stalk—need a two-year commitment. Two years isn't a long time in a garden, so if you decide you really aren't all that pleased with your biennial after two years, get rid of it. Don't let that hollyhock go to seed all over your garden, like I did with one with the double flowers in an awful peachy orange color that look like they were made of tissue paper that got rained on and turned to mush. Though, I'm surprised any bee figured out how to get beyond all those frilly petals to pollinate it so it could set seed.

Perennials require a bit more commitment. The general expectation is they will grow all summer, die back to the roots for the winter, return the following year, then repeat that cycle for years and years. Forever! Some perennials are quite good at that. But some perennials aren't. They disappear after a few years, and you are left scratching your head, wondering what you did wrong. Did you not love it enough? The truth is you might have done nothing wrong. Sometimes perennials just don't come back. Maybe they didn't grow enough roots during a previous dry summer so they had nothing to grow on the following spring. Perhaps they started to return in the spring and a late frost knocked them back too far to recover. Don't despair over one failure. If a perennial disappears one spring and you loved it, go buy it again or look for a new, improved variety of that plant. Or, use the opportunity to fill the hole it left behind with a plant you love even more.

For shrubs and trees, you should spend more time figuring out which ones you really love, or at least strongly like, before you plant them in your garden because you are going to be in a long-term relationship with them. I say "should" because every gardener at some point is going to fall in love with a shrub or tree, buy it on a whim, plant it after one dance through the garden, and then spend years regretting it because it wasn't a particularly good plant for the garden or they simply planted it in the wrong place. But if you do a little research first, you won't make this mistake and you'll be happy for what you hope is a long-term relationship. You want the trees to last longer than you do and the shrubs to give you at least ten and perhaps 20 or more good years before they need to be replaced.

And what about houseplants? Buy whatever catches your eye and waves a pretty leaf at you. Will they last forever? Maybe. I have several houseplants that are over 30 years old and one houseplant, a night-blooming cereus, that has been in the family for over 50 years. It's the ugliest houseplant I have, but I love it because it's like a member of my family. Those are the exceptions. Most houseplants won't last that long but are still worth growing if you love them.

Whew. It seems like there's a lot to take into consideration when figuring out which plants you want in your garden and house! Yes, for a while you might feel like you have a revolving door of plants coming in and going out of your garden as you figure out which ones you love. That's perfectly fine and acceptable and part of the process of becoming and being a gardener. I promise, eventually you'll end up with a garden filled with plants you love.

7
LOVE THE PLANTS YOU CAN GROW

Save yourself the heartache of replacing plants over and over by loving the kinds of plants that grow well in your garden.

Woe unto those gardeners who fall in love with plants that won't grow in their gardens. Even more woe unto such gardeners when they try to grow that plant in their gardens anyway.

How does this happen, anyway? People and plants move around. That's how it happens. Let's say, for example, that someone grows up in the Midwest where spring means peonies, lilacs, and lilies of the valley. Then they move to the deep south, maybe all the way south to New Orleans. Now they can grow camellias and jasmine vines. They can have a palm tree in their backyard. But what they cannot have—and therefore long for—are the peonies, lilacs, and lilies of the valley from their childhood.

Or flip the move. Maybe someone who grew up in the south moves north where they yearn for camellias. Can they grow them outside? They can try to do so. Unlike the peonies, lilacs, and lilies of the valley, which require a cold winter before they can flower, camellias do not. What they need is protection from the cold. For those gardeners, there is hope, for it's far easier to provide protection from the cold than it is to provide the cold. And where there is hope, there's someone willing to try.

Thus, our southern gardener now becomes a zone pusher, trying to grow warm-zone plants in a colder climate than they usually live in. Can a zone pusher succeed? Possibly, with a little cooperation from Mother Nature providing mild winters and a lot of work on the part of the gardener to provide protection for the plant. This protection can range from actually digging up the plant and storing it in a cold basement or unheated garage, to wrapping it with burlap to protect it from the biting cold. And if they choose varieties that others have had success with in colder gardens, maybe, just maybe, they can coax a camellia to produce a flower or two in a cold climate.

Believe it or not, it's not always those who grew up in other climates who become zone pushers. People who've never moved more than a few miles from where they grew up in the Midwest can become obsessed with growing tropical plants, outside, with winter protection. Are they successful? Sometimes they are. A little bit of success with one plant, perhaps a hardy banana, just encourages them to try to grow more and more plants that no one else has successfully nurtured through the winter in their climate.

If you want to live your best gardening life, I suggest you think long and hard about the extra effort it takes to grow plants that are just—bluntly stated—not suited to your garden's hardiness zone. Think about the extra work you're adding to protect that plant, perhaps to haul it in and out of your house or garage or basement with every change of season. Consider the cost of not only purchasing that weird tropical plant or that less-than-hardy camellia but also of protecting it and having it die anyway. Now you've got something to prove, so you buy another one. And another one! Where does it end? In a compost pile filled with dead plants?

It is so much better to love the plants you can grow that thrive in your hardiness zone.

But if you find that you cannot heed this advice and still wish to push your zone, and it makes you happy to do so, and you are willing to accept the losses because of that one success, that one little camellia bloom, I wish you the best. Doing so may make your gardening life more interesting, more challenging, more exciting. It may be exactly what you consider your best gardening life. If so, I wish you Godspeed, dear zone pusher!

8

REMOVE THE PLANTS YOU DON'T LIKE

You'll lose all interest in your garden if you don't like the plants in it.

Do you know what's really hard for some gardeners to do? It's hard for them to admit they just don't like a particular plant, dig it up, and toss it out of their garden.

Maybe you don't like the ivy that covers the sides of your house—destroying it in the process— and half of your yard.

Perhaps you despise those big overgrown yews someone planted 40 years ago that must be trimmed every spring to keep them from completely obscuring your front door.

Maybe you are tired of the same old yellow daylilies.

Those boring yellow daylilies. They may be the common 'Stella D'Oro' daylilies that came to fame around 1975 with a promise of a long season of bloom. Today we see those daylilies in plantings at the local office park, the shopping mall, the gas station, and up and down neighborhood streets. Those daylilies are everywhere, and you've decided you no longer like them because "they aren't all that." Good. Of all the examples I listed, they will be the easiest to remove from your garden. A couple of good digs with a shovel, and they should pop right out. Then you can give them away or compost them. But remember, even in the compost, those daylilies may continue to grow.

Good luck with the ivy and yews. It won't be easy to break up with ivy and yews and many other plants you have in your garden that you no longer love. Removing them will be like getting a messy divorce. You'll probably need professional help if you want to have any chance of a successful, amicable parting of ways because the yews will be huge and the ivy will be well-rooted.

Of course, it's much easier to get rid of a plant that you personally didn't buy and plant, and I mean "mentally easier" because it may still take a Herculean effort— plus heavy equipment you don't always find in the average garden shed—to actually remove all that ivy or those overgrown shrubs.

But if you did plant something big—or something that grew big when you weren't looking—and now it turns out you don't like it, it's still better to get rid of that plant than to suffer silently with it season after season. Yes, removing it may fill you with lament and guilt and a sense of wastefulness. The *money* you spent on those plants you don't like! What about the money? Someone else might say something about the money you spent, or maybe you'll just hear a little voice in your head whispering it to you. Wasteful. *Wasteful. Wasteful!*

Let me offer some words in your defense. Everyone buys stuff they decide later they don't like, as evidenced by clothes hanging in our closets with tags still attached. Once we got those new clothes home maybe the color wasn't what we remembered because the store lighting was weird. Maybe it didn't fit quite right when we tried it on again a month later because our weight had changed. Or even though it was a lovely shirt or pair of pants or jacket, we never had the proper occasion to wear it.

The same thing can happen with plants. That bloom color

that looked so great in the garden center turned out to be more coral than pink and clashed with the other flowers around your garden. Or, you misread the tag and realized the shrub was going to grow five feet across and you only gave it three feet to grow in, thinking all along you'd keep it pruned so it wouldn't get so big. Then you didn't prune it for several years, and behind your back, it grew to six feet tall and wide.

Maybe after you brought the plant home, as much as you tried, you just couldn't find a good spot for it. So, you let it languish in its container on the patio hoping that one day the right spot for it would just open up in the garden. You thought the sun would one day magically shine on that area, calling your attention to it so you'd see it and exclaim, "Ah ha! That's the perfect spot for it!" But that never happened, and the poor plant gave up and died.

You have my permission to get rid of *all* those plants. The plants that turned out to be the wrong color, the wrong size, and just plain wrong for your garden. The plants you inherited from a previous owner of your garden and now hate.

Donate them to someone who will love them.

Compost them.

Just get rid of them.

Do it now rather than later because the sooner you remove the plants you don't like and replace them with plants you love, the better your gardening life will be.

9
BEWARE OF FREE PLANTS

Free plants can be thugs disguised as gifts and can take over your garden if you aren't careful. Do be careful.

"I HAVE SO many of this plant, please take all you want." If someone says this to you, do not, under any circumstances, accept their kind offer. Ask instead why they have so much of that plant in the first place, so much that they are offering for you to take all you want.

I'll tell you why they have so much of that plant that they are willing for you, or anyone, to take all you want. It is because that plant is likely a thug, a rampant self-sower, a plant that will not stop until it has taken over your entire garden. It has already taken over your friend's garden, and now it has its roots set on taking over yours.

And shame on that other gardener for offering you that plant. Why, if they have so much of it, would they want to curse you with it as well?

On the other hand, if someone says, "I don't have much of this plant and it is so hard to find for sale, but I would love for you to have it for your garden," you should strongly consider accepting their generous offer. By doing so, you may be helping to propagate a plant that otherwise might die out. The plant's very survival may rely on you taking it, planting it, nurturing it, and growing it to a size that allows you to plant it forward by offering part of it to yet another gardener. It's practically unthinkable for you to not take that plant! Even if you think you might kill that plant, you should at least try to grow it.

Remember that every plant offered from one gardener to another gardener falls somewhere between these two extremes.

How will you know if you should accept a free plant?

The best thing to do, if it is possible, is to go to the garden where the proffered plant is already growing. Do you see it everywhere? No? That is a good sign that it is a plant worth graciously accepting.

Yes, it is everywhere? Back away! Run away! Do not look back! Do not take that plant, even a tiny piece of a root of it! Wipe down your pants legs to make sure no seed or tiny bit of it is clinging to you! You do not want that plant in your garden!

The general generosity of most gardeners does take some getting used to. No gardener wants you to leave their garden empty handed. They insist you take a plant or two home with you. Or a little packet of seeds they collected. Or, if they grow vegetables and it is the right time of year, they load you up with squash and tomatoes, maybe even sneaking an extra summer squash, or two, or a dozen, into the trunk of your car while you aren't looking.

Of course, that does create a tiny conundrum for you if don't want the particular plant growing in your garden, or you don't care to eat those vegetables. If that is the case, honesty is the best policy, as always. Perhaps suggest to the person other ways they can give those plants or vegetables away. Go online and post about the free plants. Offer the vegetable to a food pantry. Even put them out front with a sign advertising them for free.

Free plants! Free food! They are part of a gardening tradition that goes back for generations. Keep the tradition alive. Accept free plants. Offer free plants. Help pass on one of the best things about living a gardening life. Free plants! (And sometimes, free food!)

I do want to add a footnote of sorts here. There are some people who, desiring a plant from another gardener's garden, have been known to snag a mature seed head or snip off a little stem to root when they thought no one was looking. Or worse, while the owner's back was turned, they just outright dug a part of a plant out, roots and all. *Don't do this.* It's stealing! That plant will never grow right in your garden because it was stolen. And if it did, it would be a monument to your dishonesty. No one wants that in their garden! Not if they are planning to live their best gardening life.

❧ 10 ❧

TRY NEW PLANTS

New plants come on the market every year, and some of them deserve to be in your garden.

IF YOU'VE GARDENED for a while, this piece of advice—try new plants—is going to seem like advising someone to keep breathing. New plants? Of course. What gardener doesn't want to grow the latest and greatest varieties?

New plant varieties come out every single year. Remember that purple-flowering Wave petunia we all clamored for when it first came out in the late 1990s? Maybe you don't remember it if you are too young, or too new to gardening, or garden in the desert. Believe me, it made a big splash in the gardening world.

Back then, we were all wild to get the new Wave petunias, even though they only came in purple, because they kept blooming and growing without having to be deadheaded. Miracle petunias! Not your father's fussy, messy petunias that had to be deadheaded to keep flowering. The ones that always left your fingers kind of sticky when you pinched off old flowers.

Now there are at least six kinds of Wave petunias: Cool Wave, Shock Wave, Easy Wave, Tidal Wave, Double Wave, and of course, plain ol' Wave. The colors range from white to pink to purple and all shades in between. Every year, it seems like there's a new variety or color of Wave petunia. There are so many that it is sometimes hard to find an ordinary, original, now old-fashioned Wave petunia.

Where was I before I took off on that tangent about Wave petunias? Oh, yes. New varieties. They come out every year. Annuals that grow for just one season are worth trying, because that new plant may truly be the next big thing. You'll be the cool, with-it gardener on your block who has them! Of course, they may turn out to be a flash in the garden, and everyone will move on to something else next season. And, if those annuals turn out to be a bust, you haven't lost too much, and you can quickly move on.

With perennials, trying the new varieties is also a good idea but since you are hoping these plants will return each year, you should do a little more homework to be sure the new variety is growing up to its expectations in other people's gardens. If those new perennials are good, they'll come back to the garden centers the next year. You can certainly roll the dice and buy them the first year, but you won't be too far behind if you wait a year.

For tree and shrubs, new varieties can be a bit trickier because you really are making a long-term commitment and probably spending a bit more money, too. It's not going to be like dating some cheap annual for a year! It's not even like going steady with a perennial for a few years. With trees and shrubs, you are going to have them around for a good long time. You are marrying them! Getting rid of them will not be so easy should you decide they were a huge mistake in your life. So, do more homework and ask more questions to make sure you and that new tree or shrub variety are compatible before you make a commitment to it.

That's my advice for marriage—oops, I mean living your best gardening life.

II

KEEP SOME OLD PLANTS

Don't turn your back on last year's varieties or even older plants. Many are still around because they are simply good plants.

THE OPPOSITE of gardeners chasing after the latest and greatest variety are those gardeners who are trying to grow only old varieties. Why do they want the old varieties? Maybe they want a shrub just like grandma had in her garden, the one she called a snowball bush. Or they want a good old-fashioned beefsteak tomato, the kind their dad grew and their mom served with nearly every meal in the summertime. That homegrown, old-fashioned beefsteak tomato tastes just like what a tomato should taste like.

Or perhaps they long for a large, shady patch of lily of the valley, which has a scent that takes them back to when they were children picking those dainty bell-like flowers at their grandma's house every spring.

That could be me.

I suppose there could also be someone who lives in an older house, maybe one built in the 1920s, and, to be authentic in its restoration, they only want plants that would have been around when the house was built. So, they seek out a daylily called 'Hyperion' which was a new variety around 1925. Okay, maybe that example is a little far-fetched, but that daylily variety is still around, still growing, and still one of the best yellow daylilies to grow, in my opinion.

Whatever our reasons for choosing old varieties over new varieties, or vice versa, we should keep in mind that as new varieties are introduced to gardeners, it doesn't necessarily mean that the old varieties are no good anymore or that the new varieties are superior. Sometimes, new varieties are just new, although they might have improved disease resistance, or bigger flowers, or are smaller than the old varieties.

In the vegetable garden, better disease resistance in new tomato varieties might be a good reason to switch from an old heirloom to that new variety, especially if your old tomato plants seem to wither and the vines succumb to blight by Labor Day. And how about sweet corn? It's almost impossible to find older varieties of sweet corn because newer varieties are sweeter, and we've been told our modern taste buds probably wouldn't like those older varieties anyway.

But in some cases, older varieties still haven't been beaten by new varieties. In fact, they have become the standard by which all other varieties are measured and fall short. I offer one humble example. 'Cherry Belle', a radish variety, won an All-America Selections award in 1949 and still hasn't been bested by new varieties, in my radish-growing opinion.

I offer more evidence with a shelling pea variety called 'Green Arrow'. Shelling peas take a lot of work to shuck once they are ripe. Some varieties, which shall not be named, offer just two or three or four measly peas in a pod. It hardly seems worth the effort to pick them and shell them out. I don't care if they taste better, a pod with a stingy amount of peas in it is simply not worth the effort. That's why, year in and year out, no matter what new pea varieties come on the market, I always make room for a row of 'Green Arrow' peas. Tried and true, with eight, nine or more peas in a pod, they are worth the effort. But I'm always willing to try another row of a new pea variety, just to see and compare and perhaps be converted.

It sounds like I've made a case for sticking with old varieties. Actually, my case is never to be a snob about the vintage of plants one prefers. It can be easy to become one of those gardeners who are chasing the elusive "newer, better, faster, stronger, fancier" varieties. But don't forget to plant some old varieties, too, for nostalgia, for taste, because you like them, or maybe sometimes because they simply are better.

12
SOW SEEDS

Sowing seeds is one of the most gratifying acts of gardening and often one of the easiest things to do.

I ONCE WENT through the checkout lane at a big box store with a little clutch of seed packets. As the young cashier scanned each packet she asked me with a straight face, "Do these things really work?" I replied with a simple, "Yes, they do." But, in my mind, I was wondering what in the world they were teaching or not teaching kids these days. Where did she think plants came from if seeds didn't work? Had she ever planted a garden with actual seeds? Did she even know what a garden was? Or where her vegetables came from?

What must life be like for someone who doesn't know that seeds actually do work?!

If you want to live your best gardening life, you really should learn to grow some plants from seeds. Why? Because some plants grow best in your garden if you start with seeds. Plus, you'll open up a whole new world of plant possibilities if you sow some seeds. Not to mention that plant for plant, growing plants from seeds is usually cheaper in the long run.

Okay, I'll admit if you add in the cost of a seed starting station made with some sturdy metal shelves, grow lights on timers, optional heat mats, seed flats, soil, and peat pots, plus the actual seeds, you might not end up with cheaper plants. However, if you keep reusing your seed starting station, over time the cost goes down. Truth be told, you don't need all of those things to successfully grow seeds.

But let's go back to the new world of plant possibilities and forget about economics. For many vegetables, like peppers and tomatoes, the number of varieties to choose from goes up considerably if you start your own plants from seeds. You will be living the dream with the varieties you want. You won't be locked into the mundane existence of those gardeners who go out in the spring to buy whatever varieties the local garden centers have for sale that year.

Some plants just like it better if you sow them where they are actually going to grow. Like corn, sunflowers, and zinnias. And marigolds, for starters.

The good news for everyone is that seed companies have a vested interest in you being successful with your seed sowing and growing. They want you to be a satisfied customer so you'll buy more seeds. Instructions on the seed packets tell you how deep to plant the seeds, how far apart to space them, and whether you should sow them where they will eventually grow or start them inside first.

In even more good news, most of the seeds you are likely to buy are pretty easy to sow. Sow and water. Of course, there are some seeds that need a little extra care before they grow. Perhaps they will need to be refrigerated for several weeks before sowing. This process goes by the big word stratification. Or maybe they need to be passed through a bird's innards before they'll germinate, which you will never be able to make happen so you rough those seeds up with a little sandpaper instead. We call that scarification.

Some plants are pyrophiles. The seeds actually won't germinate until they feel the heat from a fire. Fortunately, the likelihood of you ever trying to grow any seeds that require you to heat them up—simulate a forest fire—is pretty low. Sorry to disappoint the pyromaniacs who thought I was offering them an excuse to get out the matches.

Anyway, let's not get ahead of ourselves with seeds. We just have to know that seeds work—they definitely work—and there are almost always instructions on the packet to tell you what to do. Follow those instructions and step into a whole new world of plant possibilities and a whole new gardening life.

13
GARDEN WITH STYLE

When you adopt a style, suddenly it all starts to look less like a hodge-podge of plants and more like a garden.

HAVE you ever noticed what toddlers look like when they dress themselves for the first time? They pick out all their favorite articles of clothing and end up with one or two shirts that don't exactly match their pants. They put on a pair of shorts over their pants, and sometimes a tutu, too, because it just feels right to them. Then they add two mismatched socks and a hat that was really intended to be worn only on Halloween. Now they are ready to face the world, confident in their selections.

Some gardens look like that. Many gardeners choose plants they like and put them all together, even though they might not be the best pairings. Then, just as a toddler learns which pants match which shirts and begins to gravitate to one style or another as they grow, new gardeners gradually shape their gardens into a style they like as their knowledge of plants and gardening grows.

And there are many styles of gardens!

There's the "plant it and forget it" style which really isn't a gardener's style but is typically the style of someone who is misguided and doesn't want to mess around with plants. The other extreme is the garden of "I never met a plant I didn't want and get" which is filled to the edges, and sometimes beyond, with a lot of plants. Dare we say too many plants? Variations of this garden include ones that are filled to overflowing with only a particular type of plant, perhaps daylilies or roses. Only the gardener knows the difference between that red one over there and the other red one on the other side.

Another variation is the plant collector's garden. He or she fills their garden with the most exotic, rare, unusual plants they can find. Or maybe they have a goal to grow every type of geranium they can find. Often, they stick plant labels all over the place, too, to help them keep it all straight and to remind visitors that this is not just a garden, *This is a collection!*

Some gardeners adopt a native plants style and seek out only those plants that are indigenous to their area. This is limiting, as is any adherence to a particular style, but if done well does rise above the level of a field, or woods, or a desert, depending on your location.

Other gardeners like whimsical gardens. Whimsy is sometimes hard to define, but when you see it, you know "whimsy" is just the right word to describe it. In these gardens you might find lots of nooks and crannies that look like the perfect hiding place for a garden fairy or two. Maybe you see a bird cage filled with flowers hanging from a tree.

We could go on with garden style descriptions. There are English cottage gardens, prairie style gardens, Italian villa style gardens, woodland gardens, and everything in between. Some people even have a big enough garden that they can have different styles in different areas.

The good thing about garden styles is that, just as in fashion, there are no hard and fast rules. There are trends. There are seasons. There are phases we all go through. The most important thing for the gardener intent on living their best gardening life is to style their garden however it feels right to them.

Yes, I know some gardeners lack the confidence to design their garden in the style they want, or just don't know where to start. That's where a garden designer can help. A good garden designer can help you plan a garden that fits your style. They can guide you toward smart plant purchases so you can skip the expensive step of buying all the wrong plants and then having to replace them. They can come to your garden, take you by the hand, and lead you toward a better gardening life.

14
CHANGE WHAT YOU DON'T LIKE

Nothing in a garden is permanent, so change it if you don't like it.

THERE IS nothing permanent in gardening, except that which is permanent because of constraints of time, money, and heart. So, if you don't like something in your garden, and you have the right amount of time, money, and heart, you can change it.

Fortunately, many small changes can go a long way to improve a garden and the life we spend in that garden. Simple changes, such as widening a garden border to get rid of an awkward angle, can make it nicer to mow.

Let's say you've got a flower border with a blurred line of grass that creeps into it. With a nice V-shaped cut along its edge to show where the grass ends and the border begins makes any garden border, no matter how messy or weedy or overgrown it is, suddenly look a little better.

We can also change a garden by cutting back an overgrown shrub, that one that smacks us in the face every time we walk past it. Maybe it hides too much of the house. We've all driven by houses that have been swallowed up by shrubs that have grown so big it is no longer obvious where the front door to the house is, if we even realize there is a house behind those shrubs.

Once your garden looks a little better, you might be inspired to make it look a lot better with some editing.

Just what is garden editing, anyway? Editing is just as important in gardening as it is in writing. Small edits, like removing spent flowers and plants and adding new plants, can go a long way to improving the looks of a garden. And big edits, like cutting out that shrub that is way too big, can make amazing improvements.

Sometimes it's hard for the gardener to see the edits that would help make the garden look better, just like it is difficult for a writer to edit her own writing. Invite another gardener over to see your garden with fresh eyes to suggest changes you can make. If you don't know a gardener or know a gardener you trust, look for a garden coach or garden designer and pay them a little money to suggest changes that might make your garden and your gardening life better.

Editing sometimes means digging up and dividing perennials that have become crowded and then replanting them somewhere where they have a little more room to grow. Another benefit of digging and dividing is more free plants for elsewhere in your garden or to share with a friend. (As long as they aren't thuggish free plants. Please review the chapter *Beware of Free Plants*.) Sometimes editing means digging up an entire plant and moving it someplace else in the garden where it might look better or grow better. And sometimes, yes, it means digging up a plant and getting rid of it entirely.

Many gardeners get a little squeamish when it comes to digging and dividing plants or severely pruning them back. This is where heart comes in. In your heart, you know you are doing a good thing overall, even though it looks like you are destroying that plant. Just remember, it usually takes a lot to kill a plant, so what you are doing may look destructive but in the long run you'll end up happy with the changes you've made and happier with your garden overall.

One other piece of advice on changing what you don't like in your garden: Once you decide to change something, go ahead and make that change as long as it is the right season to do so. Pruning a spring-flowering plant in the fall is likely to remove the buds for those spring flowers. Digging and dividing perennials in the middle of summer is likely too stressful for even the toughest plant.

If it's the right season, and you're ready, make those changes to live your best gardening life.

(By the way, even if it isn't the right season but it's your only chance to transplant, go ahead and do it anyway.)

15

PLANT FOR THE LONG TERM

Plant for the future, not just for the here and now.

WHEN IS the best time to plant a tree?

Some people answer that question with autumn, which is the best season to plant a tree, for the most part. There are exceptions. There are always exceptions, which is why gardening isn't a "follow the rules" kind of hobby.

The other answer to that question is 20 years ago because then you get to enjoy the tree when it is more or less at its prime. That's why some of the first plants you should purchase when you have a new garden are the trees, assuming your garden will have trees. If you are blessed with a garden with older trees in it, you should do all you can to protect the health of those trees, including consulting with an arborist if a tree looks like it has any problems.

But planting trees isn't all I am referring to when I tell people to plant for the long term. I also mean spacing and giving plants room to grow to their full potential.

I see crowded plantings all the time. Someone buys little

shrubs and plops them in the ground about a foot apart from one another. That first year it looks nice. But then, a few years later, the shrubs have grown and maybe not even grown that much. They look crowded, maybe even sickly, because they are competing for space. We know there are laws of physics at work here—two objects cannot occupy the same space at the same time—and since laws like that can't be easily broken, one or both of the plants struggles.

If only the gardener had looked at the tag and realized that each plant was going to grow three feet wide. Then the plants could have been spaced three feet apart and given room to grow. Sure, it might look a bit sparse for a year or two or three after planting, but once those shrubs start growing, they'll fill in, be properly spaced, and look great.

That's what planting for the long term really means. Think about the mature size of the plant, and give it enough room to grow to its mature size. It may look a little underwhelming at first, but eventually when those plants grow up you are going to stand back and comment, "I'm sure glad I planted for the long term."

Remember, there are always exceptions to the rules. One of these exceptions is when you are planting seasonal flowers—mostly annuals—in containers. Pack them in there. Don't worry if the label says to plant them one foot apart. Sure, you need to give them some room but not nearly as much room as if you had lined them up in a garden bed. Smash them in that container a little tighter so the container looks filled out. That's how you end up with a beautiful over-the-top arrangement, the kind that knocks the trowel right out of your hand when you see it. When that happens, you know you are living your best gardening life.

Oh, and here is a footnote about houseplants. Don't plant small houseplants in gigantic containers hoping one day they will be big enough to fill that container. Nope. Plant houseplants in a container that is appropriate to their size when you pot them up. Then, as they grow, keep putting them in increasingly bigger pots until one day they are big enough for that big container you wanted them to be in all along.

Gardening. Just when you thought you had it all figured out, along come rules and exceptions to rules, plus sometimes the need for a tape measure. All necessary, of course, when you decide to up your gardening game and live your best gardening life.

16
PRUNE WITH GOOD CUTS

Good pruning can make all the difference, as can bad pruning, so learn some simple rules of cutting back.

WHOLE BOOKS HAVE BEEN WRITTEN about pruning, and I'm going to give you the gist of it in one single chapter of well less than a thousand words. Sharp tools and proper timing. That's it. You're welcome!

For those who want just a little bit more information, but not much more, here it is.

Removing dead flowers is generally a good idea with annuals and perennials. We call it deadheading. Yes, I wish it had another name but no one has come up with a better one so far. For some plants, cutting off the fading flowers encourages them to grow more flowers because their whole goal in life is to flower, get pollinated, and form seeds for the next generation. When those seeds don't form because you nipped off the dead flowers with a pruner or your fingers, the plant tries again by producing more flowers.

However, for vegetables, this principle of cutting off spent blooms right away doesn't apply. Instead, you wait for the fruit to form, then pick off the fruit. And yes, I am using the term fruit in the botanical sense as the seed-bearing part of the plant. You want that squash plant to keep producing squash. You want that tomato plant to keep pumping out flowers and tomatoes. Keep picking the squash. Keep picking the tomatoes. That plant will keep trying, and trying, and trying, and you'll eat, and eat, and eat until you are sick of whatever it is you are picking, or frost finally kills off the plant.

Other plants—tulips for example—only have one flower per year and no amount of deadheading is going to force that plant to rebloom, at least not that same spring. However, you still want to cut off the spent blooms on tulips and other one-bloom wonders. Let the leaves continue to grow until they've turned brown because this encourages the plant to grow a bigger bulb and become a stronger plant for the next year instead of wasting all its energy producing seeds.

More pruning advice:

Dead branches should always be removed.

Trees should never be topped.

No pruning should be done when plants are frozen.

Another good rule of thumb when pruning is to always cut back a branch as close to the main stem as possible so you don't leave little stubs of the branch where they can rot off. If you are pruning to shape the plant, try to cut to the top of the next bud or leaf. This doesn't apply to shrubs that you shear, like boxwood. Goodness, it would take you forever to prune every stem individually and precisely on a boxwood or yew or other topiary type of shrub.

Speaking of shearing, there is another kind of pruning called rejuvenation pruning. This involves cutting a plant back, often a shrub, to the point you think you've surely killed it, but then it comes back nicer and fuller. I do this all the time with spireas and other shrubs of that ilk. The trick is to whack them back in early spring right before they break dormancy.

One last thought on pruning. To shape or not to shape? Are you going to be one of those people who tries to prune his forsythia into a nice round ball or a square with sharp corners? Or are you going to be one of those people who lets a shrub grow to its natural shape and size? Let me give you a piece of advice. Pick the right size shrub and let it grow to its natural shape and size. It will be prettier in the long run, and you'll save yourself hours of pruning.

As I noted at the beginning of this chapter, entire books have been written on pruning and how best to do it. I've whacked the whole topic down to nubbins here, but hopefully it is enough information for you to realize pruning plants is a little science, a little art, and some style, too. Find a book, find a mentor, and learn over time when and how to prune the plants in your gardening world.

17
FEED YOUR PLANTS

Fertilizing plants is sometimes necessary, but do it with the long-term goal of improving the soil health.

AT SOME POINT, you'll look at your plants and decide they look pale, or they aren't growing as fast as you thought they should grow. Or they just look puny. If that's the case, and it eventually will be the case, it's time for us to have the Fertilizer Talk. We'll start with the basics.

Most fertilizers contain three primary elements needed for plant growth: nitrogen, phosphorus, and potassium. When you look at a bag or box or bottle of fertilizer it will list the percent of those elements it contains in always the same order, N-P-K. So, which fertilizer do you need? Are bigger numbers better? Should you go with organic or inorganic fertilizer?

So many questions!

Keep in mind that when you fertilize plants, what you are actually doing is adding those elements to the soil and the plants are going to take them up from the soil. So, when your plants look like they need a little boost, you should check your soil health first. Then, based on what you find out, add the appropriate fertilizer.

At this point, I'd love to just pat you on the head and ask, "Do you understand?" and then have you nod your head because you are too embarrassed to tell me you need more information. But I'll spare us both the awkwardness and offer a bit more advice.

The primary advice most often given is this: Before you go wildly buying fertilizer to put on your ailing plants, test your soil to see what it is lacking, if anything. Armed with that information, you can decide which fertilizer is the best option. You could find out your soil isn't really lacking in N-P-K but has other problems, like it is too alkaline or too acidic, which would necessitate other action. Go back to the chapter on soil to find out more about testing your soil.

I do have good news for you if you are growing plants in containers using commercial potting soil. You can just go right ahead and fertilize those plants because the constant watering of those containers ensures that the elements needed for plant growth are getting flushed out regularly, assuming you have good drainage holes in those pots. If you don't have good drainage in those containers, we have to have another kind of talk!

Anyway, you can go right ahead and fertilize plants in containers without getting that potting soil tested first. Keep in mind the general guidelines that high nitrogen is great for foliage and high potassium helps to produce flowers. But don't get too hung up on that information. Most of the fertilizers on the market today have good labeling to tell you what they are good for. Buy one of those based on the plants you have and feed your container plants.

Remember that sometimes a pale, puny plant might appear sick because it isn't getting enough nutrients from the soil. But it could also be too crowded in a container, or it isn't getting enough sun, or you really are overwatering it. There may be other reasons your plants are puny that are too much to get into in this one little book. Just know that more fertilizer might not be the answer. Or it might be.

Now, aren't you glad we had this talk about fertilizer? At this point, you are probably going to tell me about all the gardeners you know who haven't had their soil tested and are using fertilizers. Wink, wink. I know. It's possible that what they are doing is good, and it's also possible they are wasting their money. Hard to say without some soil testing and a look-see around their garden. The best advice is still to occasionally have your soil tested, especially if you feel like your plants just aren't growing as well as they should.

If you have any more questions about feeding your plants, and as you garden more you will have more questions, you are going to have to do some research on your own. Fortunately, there is a lot of good information out there once you go looking for it. Just make sure you are looking at reliable sources (reliable sources don't reference common household products) and remember, your garden often doesn't need as much fertilizer as you might think.

18
WATER YOUR GARDEN

Few gardeners get all the rain they need, so make plans to water your garden when needed.

It is a fact of gardening that, at some point, you will have to water your plants.

I once helped an old neighbor with what turned out to be the last vegetable garden he planted before moving to a retirement home. He wasn't going to plant a garden that spring because he knew he wasn't physically able to do so and would be moving by the end of the summer, but I talked him into it. We planted tomatoes, green beans, acorn squash, and sweet corn, and watered it all in. Then we waited for the rain. Which never came. It turned out to be the drought year of all drought years.

Now, if it had been just me and my garden, I would have watered. I did water my own garden. But I don't think my old neighbor was one to do a bunch of watering. He grew up on a farm where, once you planted, you had to live with the rain Mother Nature sent you. So, his garden languished. At the point when the corn should have been three feet tall, it was struggling along at a straggly six inches. And everything else looked much worse.

Fortunately, we laughed about it later and admitted it was the worst garden either of us had ever planted.

The lesson in all this is that when you plant a garden expecting a certain amount of rainfall—the normal rainfall for your area—and you don't get it, you should expect to water some. Or, if you plant a garden and know you won't get enough rain in your climate for it to grow, you are obligated to water it. Otherwise, all was for naught.

Of course, we expect to water container plants, our captive plants. They rely on us. And we plan accordingly.

We now turn our attention to that love-hate relationship that every gardener has with their garden hose. In the spring, we optimistically buy a big, heavy hose that is guaranteed to last a lifetime and never kink. When we see that hose, all wrapped up on the store shelf, we believe those claims.

We hoist it off the shelf and drop it with a thud into our shopping cart. We are so happy to finally be buying the last garden hose we'll ever need. It is the one. We just know it. It says it right on the cardboard circle attached to it. This hose is going to be different and better than all the other hoses.

Then we get it home and discover what bad manners it has. Kink? Of course, it will kink the minute we look at it and even think about watering with it. Heavy? So heavy we can barely stand the thought of pulling it around the garden to water. Especially when it is hot and dry and the plants really need the water. It gets heavier on those days, if that is possible. Leakproof? Did we even notice whether it was guaranteed not to leak before we bought it? Regardless, leak it shall, right where we hold it to water, thus soaking us more than the plants.

And will it ever drape nicely over the cute hose rack we bought for it or wind up straight on the fancy hose reel? Nope. It has no intention of ever looking as nice and neatly rolled up as it was on the store shelf. In fact, it might even start to unroll itself in the car as we are driving it home if one of the flimsy ties holding it in place comes undone.

Finally, just as we are fed up with this hose—just like we were fed up with all the other hoses we ever bought—it will spring a leak and send a fountain of water up into the air and straight down on us. It shows no respect.

What is the answer?

My answer is to buy as lightweight a hose as I can find and never, ever commit to a long-term relationship with it. I am committing to it for just one season at a time. Maybe longer if the hose behaves. This works for me! Perhaps it puts the hose on notice that all that bullying and taunting from those big heavy hoses will not be tolerated, and so it behaves nicely.

Plus, at even the hint of it misbehaving, I start to scroll through the Internet looking at ways to recycle garden hoses into floor mats. That shows my hose who's in charge!

Your hose mileage may vary. Just remember to keep your plants watered when Mother Nature turns off the spigot during the growing season. And water deeply each time you water. Don't just wet the soil and call it good. Deep watering less often will force those roots down for moisture, making the plants grow stronger and be healthier. And that's what every gardener wants.

19
RIGHT-SIZE YOUR GARDEN

Plant a garden that is the size you can tend. Size is determined not only by square feet but by the time, money, and strength you have.

I WAS SHOCKED when a co-worker commented that a house she and her husband considered buying was perfect except for one feature. It had "too much garden." This concept of "too much garden" was foreign to me, a much younger me who couldn't imagine having "too much garden." But this woman and her husband simply "did not garden" and realized that they would have to garden if they bought this house that was perfect except for having "too much garden."

I had to go off by myself a bit to think about these concepts of "too much garden" and "did not garden." After much thought, I realized that a more positive spin to put on it was that it just wasn't the right size of garden for them. Size matters in gardening. And size is not something measured in square feet. It is something that is measured using an equation of sorts. Square footage of the garden plus the types of plants in the garden plus the time one wants or can put into tending the garden divided by the physical strength of the person who is going to do most of the work equals the size garden one should have.

Got that? In other words, the size of your garden should be based on the resources you have to tend the garden.

If the garden is bigger than the resources available, then it soon becomes a weedy mess and begins to revert back to the wilderness it once was, or worse, a wilderness now inhabited by a variety of plants that just look untended in a way that a real wilderness doesn't. If this describes your current garden, there are many strategies you can employ to reduce the resources your garden actually needs.

You can start with the plants. Back in the Victorian Age, rich people used to bed out hundreds, if not thousands, of annual flowers in an elaborate design and then carefully monitor those plants, pinching them and cajoling them throughout the growing season to maintain the chosen design. Then in the fall they would rip them all out. If you do not employ a dozen gardeners, I suggest that bedded out annual plants à la the Victorian Age is not a suitable planting scheme for your garden.

Instead, consider a design that includes trees, shrubs, grasses and other plants that require little care except for maybe a bit of pruning once a year. Maybe add some perennials that ask nothing more than a late fall or early spring cutting back. Keep your garden palette simple. Better to have a swath of lovely coneflowers than the dottiness of one of these and one of those, and a pinch of this and a pinch of that, which tends to make most people nervous and jittery.

And one should not be nervous and jittery in a garden, at least not because of the flowers.

Maybe you long for homegrown vegetables but the mere thought of having to plow your land each spring and shape new rows is beyond what you have the strength to do. After all, who has a team of oxen and a strapping farm hand to guide those beasts and a plow through the garden? Don't despair. You can build a few raised beds which, when properly constructed, shouldn't require too much to keep them weed-free and ready to plant in the spring without having to till up the ground. In fact, to ease your mind, let me tell you the good news that tilling up the soil each spring in your vegetable garden is no longer considered to be a good practice for a variety of reasons related to soil health.

Conversely, if your garden is smaller than the resources you have available—which is possible—then you may soon become frustrated because you can't buy all the plants you want or spend as much time as you would like gardening. Well, you could buy all the plants you want but then where will you plant them? You can't just leave them in their nursery pots and let them languish on your patio. Eventually, the plants die if not planted out. If you are that unfortunate person who has a garden that's too small, your choices include moving to a bigger garden or doing volunteer gardening somewhere else. Or make your garden bigger by helping your next-door neighbors with their gardens, with their permission, of course.

Periodically, because circumstances can change, take stock of your resources—time, space, and physical ability—to size your garden appropriately. Then plan and plant accordingly to live your best gardening life.

20

CONQUER WEEDS

Every gardener battles weeds. Arm yourself appropriately.

THE MOST OFTEN-ASKED question by new gardeners is, "Is this a weed?" As soon as they see a plant they don't recognize, they snap a picture with their phone, pull up an app to post their blurry pic to an online social media group, and then ask the world what the plant is. Ugh. Is this a weed? Insert a picture of pokeweed which has to be the most common plant for which people seek identification. Is this a weed? Insert a picture of any plant as a seedling.

So many people are afraid they will pull out a plant, then find out it was a fabulous plant. And now they've killed it.

Such fear has no place in the garden.

Want to know the simple trick with weeds? Actually, two tricks.

The first trick is not to worry too much about whether a plant is a weed or not when you are weeding. Just ask, "Did I plant this?" If the answer is no, then ask the follow-up question, "Is this a self-sower from something I planted that I want to keep now?" If the answer to both questions is no, it's a weed by the definition of "a plant you don't want."

The second trick is to pull weeds when they are small. Then they aren't well-rooted and are easy to grasp between your thumb and finger. Those hapless weed seedlings should come out of the ground with just the slightest tug.

But as we've already learned, there are exceptions to every rule. This is where gardeners, especially new ones, get tripped up with weeding.

The first exception is seedlings that you yourself planted. They are also easy to pull out with just the slightest tug. If you sow seeds—and you should when possible—you should learn what the seedlings look like so if you see a tiny plant that doesn't look like them, you can confidently pull it out.

The second exception is seedlings that you didn't sow but are desirable plants, like columbine (*Aquilegia* sp.). Now there's a cheerful self-sower if ever there was one. It produces pretty spring flowers all over my garden, then becomes a lovely plant that blends in. As a bonus, columbine is easy to pull out at just about any size.

Other self-sowers, like trees, are not so nice. They are tricky. Unbeknownst to us, tree seedlings send down a root first and then poke their little leaves above ground. Most seeds do this. It gives them a head start in life. By the time you see the oak tree or walnut or redbud or mulberry or name-your-tree seedling, it is often rooted deep enough that you need a tool to dig it out. By all means, get that tool and dig it out.

Often a tree seedling doesn't get noticed until it is several feet tall. Then as you stand there looking at it you wonder, "Is this a tree I'd like to keep? Is this a good spot for a tree? Why would a tree grow here if it wasn't a good spot for it? Maybe I should keep it. I could move it over there. Or back there. It's free, after all!" And the answer should still be no. You do not need to keep that tree. You are under no obligation, moral or otherwise, to nurture that tree seedling where it rooted itself. And no, you should also not offer to dig your tree seedling up, pot it up, and save it for someone else.

Which brings us back to the question, “Is this a weed?” I recall visiting my sister who did a nice job of weeding her flower bed and asked me to identify two lovely plants she had carefully mulched. They had sweet little yellow flowers and clover shaped leaves. So sweet. I hated to do it, but as only a sister would, I pointed out that she had done a nice job of tending wood sorrel, a weed. If you look it up, you’ll find that there is a species of wood sorrel (*Oxalis* sp.) found just about everywhere in North America.

At that point, I suppose it was her choice whether to continue to cultivate and treat it like a highly desirable plant or weed it out. (For the record, she wanted to keep it.) In my garden, it self-sows everywhere, and I am constantly pinching it out.

By the way, there are many edible weeds. Wood sorrel is one, though it is too sour for most people. Dandelions are also edible and are probably at the top of the list of weedy good eating. I’ve heard that all parts of the dandelion plant are edible—roots, leaves, and blossoms. Then there is purslane, which has been the bane of many a gardener’s life. It, too, is edible and supposedly a great source of Omega-3 fatty oils. Yum. You go first.

Now we have learned that one gardener’s weed is another’s food source, blessed self-sower, or even majestic tree. The good news is you, the gardener, can decide what to do about each and every weed in your garden. Just take my advice if you don’t want a plant or a known weed. Pull it early before it becomes well rooted and starts to dream of where it is going to throw its seeds in your garden. You’ll be glad you did.

21
EMBRACE THE INSECTS

Believe it or not, insects are signs of a healthy garden.

IF YOU LOOK it up on the internet, you will find that scientists estimate that at any one time there are 10,000,000,000,000,000,000 insects living on this earth with us. That's 10 quintillion, in case you forgot the "illions" you learned in math class back in the day. At certain times of the summer, it will seem like all 10 quintillion of those insects are in your garden. Attacking your plants. Buzzing in your ears. Alighting on your arm to drill you with their proboscis, which is what that drilling part of a mosquito is called. Of course, you are going to slap that thing dead, leaving one less than 10 quintillion insects.

I assure you, there are not quite that many insects in your garden. Not even close. Unless of course your garden is in the middle of the Amazon jungle where the insects are not only more numerous but also much larger than any I might find in my garden.

Let me just explain right now that insects are a part of any garden, along with spiders, and you should not reach for an insecticide the minute you see an insect in your garden. Put away those sprays and powders. No matter how many insects there are. Relax. Take some deep breaths, maybe with your mouth closed if you are sitting in your garden as you read this so a little gnat doesn't fly in.

Most of the time, insects will not destroy your garden. They may nibble on a plant or two. Destroy your roses. Kill off your squash vines. Worm their way into your ears of corn. But they won't destroy your garden in its entirety. Or eat you alive. Or even come close, except for mosquitoes, which can ruin a day in a garden. My sister tells me that mosquitoes kill more people than any other insect, animal, spider, beast, whatever. She says I can do the research to prove she's right. She says to tell people mosquitoes—not spiders or bees or wasps or snakes—should send them screaming inside.

Repeat after me: Insects are a necessary and welcome part of the entire ecosystem of your garden. Plant it, and they will come. They will eat and be eaten. They will live, mate, produce more insects, eat plants, eat other insects, and die. They will annoy you, pester you, infuriate you, and possibly drive you toward taking actions to kill them.

But they also perform the vital life-giving act of pollination of many of the plants in the garden. Without them, you won't get zucchini, apples, or strawberries, to name just a few of the long list of fruits we get thanks to pollinating insects. They also play a role in breaking down organic matter, which you want to have in your garden and compost pile.

My advice to you, living your best gardening life, is to take as little action toward insects as you can possibly get away with. Your "little action" might be a strong spray with the hose to knock the insects off a plant. Or setting a trap with pheromones to lure insects to their death. Or hand-picking insects off the plants before they cause too much damage. (I'm looking at you, bagworms and hornworms.) Or finding the insect's eggs on the undersides of leaves and destroying those eggs.

Only under the direst of circumstances, such as when termites have decided your house foundation is their lunch, should you resort to an insecticide to kill bugs. In that case, please get a licensed professional to apply as little insecticide as possible to get the job done.

Overall, you are going to be much happier if you adopt a live-and-let-live attitude toward insects and spiders in your garden. Educate yourself about the insects (and spiders) you see —they are fascinating—and then learn how to garden with them. It truly is the best way.

22

BUY GOOD TOOLS

You'll enjoy gardening more when you have good tools that work with you and last for years.

My dad had only basic tools for planting his vegetable garden and tending to shrubs and flowers. His tools included one trowel, one pair of pruners, one hoe (until I got him another hoe for Father's Day one year), one spade, one edger, one rototiller (shared with two other neighbors), one garden rake, and one pair of hedge trimmers, which were rarely used once he got some electric hedge trimmers. And five leaf rakes, one for each kid.

What is missing from this list of gardening tools? Well, for starters, my dad did not own a wheelbarrow until most of us had moved away. For a while we had a blue two-wheeled cart which was awful to use for hauling anything of any size. It could not be pushed forward but had to be dragged all over the yard. In fairness, a wheelbarrow can also be difficult to use if you've loaded it with something heavy and haven't balanced your load or if you set the wheelbarrow down on a slope. In either case, it will tip over. When that happens, it's best to let go of the handles and let it tip over. I know this from my own experience.

What is the real point of this description of my dad's tools? Not to give you a shopping list for tools to buy (that list would be slightly different today), but to point out that you do not need a lot of tools to garden.

The tools you use depend on the type of gardening you do. The more you garden, the more tools you may end up with. Until one day you look in your garage or garden shed and realize that you likely have the largest hoe collection in the world, which I do have and no one has ever questioned it.

You should also keep track of your tools so you don't spend your precious gardening time hunting for your gardening knife, which is an excellent tool that my dad did not have, but I believe if he had known about it, he would have had one. My dad kept track of his trowel and his one pair of pruners by putting them on the window ledge above the hose spigot in the backyard. I tend to do the same, though I have tools of all kinds on all the window ledges around the patio. And in a basket on a small table just inside the back door and on top of a storage cabinet in the garage, and on peg hooks in the garage, and on various other shelves throughout the garage. There is a tool caddy filled with miscellaneous special purpose hand tools, some of which I bought merely to try but didn't put into the regular rotation. Plus, I can't forget to mention the barrel in one corner of the garage where the really old hoes and digging forks—which people give you when they hear you like old gardening tools—stand until I decide to make something with them or give them away.

Speaking of hoes, you may not even need one to garden. You may get along fine without one. Many gardeners do. But whatever gardening tools you do use, make sure they are made to last. Then you'll enjoy using them in your garden and your love of gardening will grow accordingly.

23
CHECK YOUR GARDEN

Bad things can happen in an untended garden. They can also happen in a tended garden, but you can stop them from becoming catastrophes if you catch them early.

THERE IS a native fruit tree that grows wild in some parts of the Midwest and produces a fruit of legends. Of course, I am referring to the pawpaw tree, *Asimina triloba.* What makes it a legend is that few people have actually eaten the fruit, described as tasting like a banana mixed with a mango mixed with a pineapple. Pawpaws have never gained wide commercial appeal because the fruits don't store well and generally ripen all at once as summer turns to fall.

Knowing all of this, I decided to plant a pair of pawpaw trees, one at each end of my vegetable garden. I was delighted when after only two years, one of them had a pawpaw fruit on it.

I watched that one piece of pawpaw fruit grow, and as it came closer to the time to harvest it, I began to check it daily. I gently touched the fruit and checked its color. It was supposed to turn from greenish to yellowish and then with a gentle touch, fall into my hands when it was ripe. Each day I checked, and each day I decided "not today."

Then life got busy, as it sometimes does, and I skipped two days of checking. On that third day, I went out once again to check my pawpaw to see if it was ripe, and it was gone. Gone! I looked where it was supposed to be on the tree. I rubbed my eyes to refocus. I blinked a few times. It still wasn't there. I looked on the ground below the tree. I looked all over the garden. I never found even a half-eaten piece of pawpaw fruit. It was gone. Vanished!

Several days later I found a little pile of pawpaw seeds sitting on a big rock in my vegetable garden, as though someone had offered them as a sacrifice on an altar. Either that or they left them there to remind me again that they had beaten me to my own pawpaws.

A happy ending to this story would be if I told you that the next year more fruit appeared, and I managed to harvest a piece for myself. Well, someday, I might write that happy ending but for now the tale merely ends with the cautionary note to be diligent in checking your garden. From one day to the next, it can change.

Fruit can be stolen off a tree.

Insects can appear out of nowhere and consume a plant.

A weed can sprout and begin to wind its way around other plants.

One summer, I looked out at a large spruce tree in my garden and saw to my surprise the beginnings of a weedy mulberry tree growing up through the spruce branches. I am being kind to myself to call what I saw "the beginnings" as though the tree was a mere foot-tall seedling. This tree, when I finally noticed it, was over 15 feet tall with a base over an inch in diameter. Had I looked more closely earlier in the season I could have easily yanked this tree out as a small seedling. Instead I had to get out a small saw to chop it down.

The list of what can happen in a garden when you aren't looking goes on and on. It's endless! A plant disease can begin to spread across a branch. A tomato that seemed almost ripe one day may be split in two, or worse, have a bite taken out of it, the next day. (When you see that bite, you immediately want to check the dental records of every squirrel around to find the guilty one and punish them.) A shrub or small tree, left unprotected in the wintertime, can be girdled to death by the sharp teeth of a hungry rabbit. Overnight, tent caterpillars can devour half of a tree, just out of your reach.

Even the weather can change in a few hours, bringing torrents of rain when the radar looked clear or no rain at all when you thought for sure the radar showed clouds directly over the spot where your garden is.

Fortunately, most of these issues and the unexpected events you might experience in a garden can be handled quickly and easily if caught early and addressed right away. That's your job as a gardener, to keep your eyes and ears open, to be diligent in checking your garden daily. To get to your one piece of ripening pawpaw fruit before some other critter gets its paws on it first.

Then one day you, too, will enjoy an unusual treat. Maybe not a piece of pawpaw fruit, but something that reminds you that your garden is well worth the time and effort it takes to visit it daily. Because you won't always find problems. In fact, most of the time everything will be fine. And you may find something that delights you!

24
MULCH LOCALLY

Use organic matter as mulch, preferably your own compost, to suppress weeds and retain moisture.

WHEN I WAS a kid in the 1970s, I do not recall anyone in my neighborhood getting a load of mulch or wood chips dumped on their driveway so the gardener could spend an afternoon or several long days scooping that mulch into a wheelbarrow and carting it all around the garden to dump around the bases of trees and shrubs.

I'm not even sure when this trend of mulching started or when that first bag of mulch showed up in a garden center, but it is a common practice today. When did it begin? What is the history of mulch? That is far too deep a topic to cover in a book such as this, so here's the most basic question about mulching:

Should you mulch?

The two primary purposes of mulching are to suppress weeds and to preserve soil moisture. A secondary purpose, in the eyes of many, is to make the garden look better. We are so used to seeing mulched beds that now bare garden beds look, well, naked.

What kind of mulch should you use?

Generally speaking, the more locally sourced your mulch product is, such as your own compost, the better it is. Other than that, the product should be as unadulterated as possible. Please skip the mulches that have been dyed black or orange or brown. To many gardeners, dyed mulches look awful from the minute they are applied and then turn uglier over time as they fade, and yes, even the dyed mulches fade.

Over time, all mulch decomposes and begins to enrich the soil. Thus, one is never done applying mulch. It becomes an annual or at least biennial event to buy mulch and spread it around the garden

Compost, which can be used as a top dressing, also enriches the soil.

Compost is what you get when you pile up grass clippings, fallen leaves, and other plant matter from your garden. Over time, microbes and other creatures, including worms and insects, feed on that plant waste, turning it into nutrient-rich compost. If you want to live your best gardening life, you should definitely find an out-of-the-way, but not too-out-of-the-way, spot for a compost pile.

I should offer a warning here that making compost and doing it well can become addictive when you see how little effort is required and what results from that effort: dark, nutrient-rich compost. When you see how well plants respond when you give them compost as a top dressing, you will never have enough.

What about rocks or gravel as mulch? Yes, rocks cover the soil and suppress weeds, at least for a while. They also make it difficult to dig in that area to add new plants and pull out old plants. Without a barrier fabric of some kind, the rocks will also gradually work their way into the soil. If you attempt to mulch with a weed barrier fabric and rocks of any kind, including river rock, pea gravel, or lava rock, you will one day regret it and have a mess on your hands as you face a lot of hard work to remove it all. Or you will move away and whoever moves in will curse you for putting down all that gravel or rock over a fabric barrier. In most gardens, rocks and gravel are nothing more than loose paving with a permanence that no garden bed or gardener should ever have to endure.

The exception might be if you live in a desert or are specifically trying to grow plants that thrive in gravel. In that case, rocks and gravel probably will work quite well for you and your plants.

Of course, the optimum condition for a garden bed or border is to have a variety of desirable plants so perfectly spaced that they won't allow weeds to grow around them. Or have plantings that make weeds look so obvious it takes just a minute or two to spot those weeds and yank them out before they set seed. Then all you need to do to keep the garden in top form is to occasionally top dress it with your favorite compost.

Here's one last piece of advice on mulching: Never use landscape fabric or plastic sheeting and put the mulch on top of that. It will ruin your soil and all the organisms that live in it. The plants will languish in that ruined soil and not grow to their potential. You will forever regret doing such a thing, and we will kick you out of the world-wide gardening club. You have been warned.

25

CONTAIN ANY PLANT

Even a container planted with a single flower is a garden.

MY FIRST ACT of gardening in the spring isn't to spade up a new garden bed or till up the existing vegetable garden. In fact, the first thing I do in the spring has nothing to do with my actual in-ground garden.

The first thing I do each spring is head out to my local greenhouse and buy the first pansies and violas of the season. I do this well before any of my neighbors think it's time to do any gardening and early enough for them to think I'm nuts to be gardening so soon when it's barely spring and mostly still winter.

Then I plant those bright violas and pansies in containers.

Thus begins a season's worth of growing plants in containers, which I and many other gardeners do even when we have plenty of ground to plant in. Why do we do this? Possibilities! That's why we do it.

From the tiniest little tuft of moss in a thimble-sized pot to a small tree in a container that requires a forklift to move it, when it comes to growing plants in containers the possibilities are almost as endless as what you can do in an in-ground garden.

You can move containers around to different locations, group them together, spread them apart, switch out old containers with new containers. You can go from flea-market funky to sleek silver sophistication just by using different containers. The options and choices are limited only by your imagination and bank account.

In some cases, I plant in containers because it is easier. I grow potatoes in large fabric pots because dumping the contents of that entire pot onto a tarp and picking out all the potatoes is faster than digging the potatoes out of a garden bed. Trust me, you'll end up spearing the biggest and best potato with your digging fork when you dig it out of the ground.

I grow mint in another container because mint is a rampant runner and would soon scamper through a garden bed. But in a container, mint is generally well behaved.

And even though I have a vegetable garden, every spring I plant a cherry tomato plant in a big pot by the back door to make it easier to grab a few cherry tomatoes as a snack when I'm sitting on the patio thinking about gardening.

Which brings up another positive about containers. The good potting soil you use is easy to work with. You'll never find rocks when digging in those containers. Or big tree roots. Or big hunks of solid clay. It is all the lovely, friable potting soil you added.

I have learned a few tricks to ensure what I plant in large containers grows well. First, I don't use all new potting soil every year. Not only can buying all new potting soil every spring be an expensive habit, there is the work of buying the soil in big heavy bags, hauling it home, and dumping it into the pots. Instead, I skim off the top layer when it starts to look yucky or grayish and mix new potting soil in with what is already there.

I also never add anything to the bottom of a container as filler in order to use less potting soil. I used to do that! We all did. We'd add old aluminum soft drink cans, empty plastic nursery pots, even Styrofoam packing peanuts in a plastic shopping bag. Now, research shows that adding all that stuff didn't help and often kept too much water in the bottom of the pot. It is far better to just fill the pot up with good potting soil, top to bottom.

I also make sure the all my containers drain properly. You want the water to be able to flow out of the pot, so don't use a container without drainage holes. Don't tell yourself that you'll just make sure not to overwater to compensate for no drainage holes. That will never work! If you've found the perfect container for growing a plant in, but it has no holes, use a drill or a hammer and a big nail to add drainage holes, if you can do so without cracking the pot.

Remember that plants in pots need additional fertilizer to grow to their potential and often need daily watering, especially when it's hot outside. They are our captives. We must water and feed them more than we water and feed the plants that grow in garden beds.

So, take care of your little captives, I mean potted plants, and don't despair if your lot in your gardening life is to only grow plants in containers. It can be a good gardening life with its own rewards.

26
GARDEN INDOORS

Houseplants are fun!

Do you remember your first houseplant? Maybe it was that little seedling your teacher helped you sow way back in kindergarten or first grade. The one you refused to plant outside after you brought it home even though inside it languished and finally died because you were a kid and you forgot about it. Then you were put off by plants for life. Well, that is sad. I hope that didn't happen to you!

I am fortunate that I was raised with houseplants. By the time I reached middle school, my dad had quite a few houseplants, including a mysterious night-blooming cereus. And yes, 50 years later, I now have that same mysterious night-blooming cereus, making it the oldest plant in my indoor garden. I should mention it is also the largest, ugliest, gangliest houseplant I have. I have to keep it in a corner of the sun room because it is supported by a trellis that sits on top of its container, and the whole thing has to lean against the wall to remain upright. It's a beastly thing!

Why do I keep it?

It's family now.

Truly, anyone can grow a houseplant or two or a dozen. And everyone should. They teach us stuff, like how plants need water and light. How if you forget to water them, they might die, or they might just wilt and then pop back up after being watered. How they shouldn't be viewed as home decor, shut up in a dark room. They are living things that need light. Fortunately, some need less light than others so we can grow them even in rooms that don't have south-facing windows.

Houseplants teach us patience as we wait and watch and wonder when that moth orchid is going to bloom again, if it is going to bloom again. Here's a secret: It will bloom again. I had a friend who picked one out of the trash at his mom's retirement home, repotted it, and it rebloomed. And then he gave it to me and it rebloomed again! With blooms that lasted for months! Such a shame to toss a plant away because it finished blooming once.

What if my dad had done that with the night-blooming cereus? Then I would have missed out on years of flowers and no longer be able to claim that I own the world's ugliest houseplant. Rather, it owns me, sitting in the corner of the sunroom, greeting me each day, reminding me of my dad, of summer days spent watching it bloom. Houseplants can do that.

If you don't believe me that houseplants are fun to own and can give you years of delight, go buy one and wait for the magic. Growing them is all part of living your best gardening life.

27

DRESS FOR THE GARDEN

Wearing comfortable clothes that you don't mind getting dirty is required for good gardening.

THERE ARE several phases gardeners go through when it comes to clothes for the garden.

In phase one, our new gardener gingerly steps out into the garden wearing normal street clothes. Within minutes, they realize that gardening is a dirty business. Their jeans now have grass stains on the knees, there is mud on their shoes, and a smudge of something unknown is smeared across the sleeve of their shirt. Even though they tried to be careful and were "only going to work in the garden for a few minutes," their normal street clothes have now become by default (or dirt) their gardening clothes. If they're smart, they'll stick to this same outfit each time they garden. Otherwise, all their street clothes become gardening clothes, and they no longer have anything left to wear in polite society.

In phase two of gardening attire, our gardener realizes that gardening can be a messy, sweaty, dirty business so they don cast-off clothes that they don't mind getting dirty. Old T-shirts, jeans, even worn-out shoes become the standard attire for the garden. They can now garden with abandon and ease with no concern about how dirty their clothes become. These duds are for gardening, after all! For many people who are living a good gardening life, this is the end of their search for perfect gardening clothes. They often garden happily ever after in old clothes repurposed for gardening.

Some gardeners go on to another, perhaps higher, phase of gardening attire. They buy clothes specifically for gardening. From head to toe, they are wearing only the finest in gardening attire. For shoes, they've purchased special gardening clogs that are made of a heavy plastic that not only keep their feet dry, but are also easy to clean with just a quick hosing off. Some people have multiple pairs of gardening clogs so they can keep a pair by the front door, a pair by the back door, even a pair by the door into the garage so wherever they exit the house, they can easily slip on a pair of clogs and be out in the garden without hunting for the right shoes. It's not necessary to know how I know this to be true, but I can prove it if need be.

This gardener wears pants purchased just for gardening. Not just any pants. These have special, deep pockets perfect for holding seed packets, tools, and gloves and keeping them within easy reach while out in the garden. Plus, the pants are made from a fabric that dries quickly so if by chance our gardener tangles with a garden hose (see chapter *Water Your Garden*), they won't stay sopping wet for long. And they have pockets on the knees for knee pads. The pants are a wonder!

Our well-dressed gardener's new gardening shirt is a special UV ray-blocking shirt that helps to protect them from the sun. Ditto their hat. Not just one hat, but an assortment of hats to match any gardening occasion, whether it is a straw hat to put on for a quick jaunt out to cut some flowers or a washable wide-brimmed hat to wear when weeding and flinging dirt about.

I suggest most people start off their gardening life dressed per phase two, with old clothes they don't mind getting dirty. Later, when gardening has become a way of life, they can happily move on to the next phase of gardening attire. Then they'll never have to worry about wet feet from the garden again. That's the pinnacle of attire because everyone knows keeping your feet dry is one of the keys to living your best gardening life.

28

GARDEN THROUGH THE IMPERFECTION

There is no perfect weather, soil, location, plants, or gardener. Garden anyway.

I WATCHED them make my brick patio several years ago. They built it over three days with layers that began with heavy black plastic covered by crushed rock, then another layer of crushed rock that had a coating that made it almost like concrete, topped with a layer of the actual bricks, all covered with a special polymer sand mixture that was swept into the cracks to help it all bind together. Even someone who never gardens would know that my patio is not the ideal condition for growing plants.

Yet in the crevices between the bricks, weed seeds annually manage to send down roots and send up shoots and make quite a "grow" of it. Add to this the self-sown seeds from petunias, columbines, and my beloved violas that manage to sprout, grow, and flower, and my patio is almost its own garden border. Of course, the plants aren't particularly robust or large, but when I attempt to pull them out, they are clearly well-rooted.

All this proves that conditions do not have to be perfect for plants to grow or for someone to have a nice garden.

It definitely helps to have the proper amount of sunlight or the right kind of shade, adequate rainfall, seasonable weather, good soil, etc. for plants to reach their optimum size and vigor. But most plants will do quite well in a range of conditions.

This is clearly a good thing for gardeners, because no garden is perfect, and all gardens contain a range of conditions.

By the way, sometimes one of the best conditions to find in a garden is a microclimate, a little spot that warms up a little faster in the spring and doesn't get quite so cold in the winter. Perhaps it is sheltered by brick walls that absorb heat all day long and then radiate it all night long so the temperature in that area is never quite as cold as the rest of the garden. That might be the perfect spot to try to grow a few tender plants, to dabble in a little zone pushing.

On the other hand, there might also be a spot or two in your garden where the frost settles first. That is not the best place for a vegetable garden unless it is the only place you have with full sun most of the day. Then go ahead and plant your vegetables there but just remember to watch out for frost.

Regardless, you'll soon figure out the idiosyncrasies of your garden, where it holds water, where it dries out faster, where the sun is, where the shade is, where the good microclimates are, and where no matter what you plant there, it dies. The important thing to remember is no garden is the same throughout, and no garden has the perfect conditions everywhere.

Whew. Such a relief to know this. Now you can happily "give it a try" with a wide variety of plants. Over time, you'll figure out for your own garden what grows well for you and what is a waste of time and money.

Along the way, you'll find that in most cases, most plants will live and often multiply themselves in your gardens, because as anyone can see from the plants that grow in the oddest places, conditions really don't have to be perfect for most plants.

Fortunately, we'll all also discover as we strive to live our best gardening lives that we don't have to be perfect either. We can and will make many mistakes in our gardens. We might leave newly purchased plants in their containers without water for a few days. We might prune a shrub in the wrong season so it has no flowers the next spring. We might step on that precious new plant as we try to reach that plant just behind it so we can stake it up. The list is endless of what we might do in our imperfect state in our imperfect gardens.

But plants are resilient and will tolerate a lot of those mistakes and a wide range of conditions. And so are gardeners.

Remember that as you tend your unique, perfectly imperfect garden.

29

FIGURE OUT WHY YOU GARDEN

Figure out why you garden, but don't think too hard about it. Sometimes, it's enough to enjoy gardening for the fresh air and the scent of a pretty flower.

WHY DO YOU GARDEN? At some point, when you are exhausted from weeding, pruning, and planting, and are covered from head to toe with dirt with more work still to be done, you may ask yourself why you garden.

You'll find yourself wiping your brow to remove the sweat dripping into your eyes, leaving a muddy trail across your forehead as you gaze off into the distance wondering what led you to this madness. Even your dog knows to stay in the shade while you are out in the sun deadheading flowers or planting yet another row of green beans.

What are you seeking out there amidst the bugs and weeds? Why not change your entire garden to lawn, call a mowing service, and then sit back and relax with a good book or recline on your couch with your television tuned to a streaming service that will happily play show after show for your next binge session?

But you aren't going to do that. You're going to keep gardening, and you aren't going to think too much about why you do so. You just feel it's the right thing to do. Eventually, season after season, you'll come up with so many reasons to garden that you'll no longer ask yourself why you put up with all you encounter in your garden.

Maybe you garden for the food. You want to eat fresh, homegrown produce. You want to experience the thrill of the perfect homegrown tomato. The way to do that, of course, is to grow your own food. What power that gives you! You toss a seed into the ground, water it, and watch while a plant springs up and flowers. You anticipate that flower fading and becoming the perfect green bean.

Perhaps you garden for the flowers. No matter where you live and garden, there are countless flowers you can grow and as they flourish in your garden you might just form an emotional connection to them. Once that happens, you'll always want to grow those flowers. You won't be able to imagine your garden without seeing camellias blooming in late winter, or smelling sweet peas in late spring, or marveling at the height of a sunflower in the summertime.

You might even make the excuse that you garden for the fresh air, the exercise, and the scent of a pretty flower.

But deep down you know the why of your gardening journey is much deeper than mere food or flowers. Like the deep roots of the many plants you've added to your garden, your why is there, deep in your soul. You won't always know how many roots there are or where they go, but you'll know they are there.

You won't always know how to put that why into words, but you know it is there. You don't know where gardening will take you, but you can't imagine life before gardening or a life without gardening. You are intent on living your best gardening life.

30

A HEARTY FAREWELL, FELLOW GARDENER

Every gardener is now your friend.

WE STARTED this book with a cheery hello, so we'll end it with a hearty farewell. But it's the kind of farewell where one friend says to another, "Safe travels, we'll see each other soon!" Because I hope you now consider me a gardening friend or at least your favorite eccentric gardening aunt, one who wants you to live your best gardening life. I hope you now feel like you at least have a chance to have the garden that you've known was in you ever since you first felt the urge to sow a seed or grow a little houseplant.

Wherever we meet, if we ever meet, we shall always have gardening in common, which makes us part of a special group of people.

Before you close this book and set it nearby where you can pick it up and reread it when you'd like a little gardening boost, it's time for one more lesson.

It's time to learn how to enjoy your garden.

Look around your garden. Where are the chairs? The

benches? The table to pull up to and enjoy a meal in your garden? Surely you didn't leave those out? If you did leave them out, you need to go back and add them to your garden so you can sit for a minute, or longer, and enjoy your garden. Why? There are few people who get enjoyment solely from working in their gardens. Yes, it is a joy to garden, to be able to bend and weed, and mow one's own lawn, and plant flowers, and pick vegetables. But it's also lovely to just sit in the garden and enjoy it for what it is, however it turned out. And to do that, you need to have chairs and benches, preferably in some shade.

Then imagine that I'm there with you, your eccentric gardening aunt, your best gardening friend, admiring all the work you've done, all the beautiful plants you've selected, all the special little touches you've added to make the garden your own. I'll nod with approval and tell you how you've done a wonderful job. Because you have done a wonderful job, and you are doing all you can to live your best gardening life.

I might also sneak in a tiny bit of advice along with the praise, mostly the advice in this book. It will be offered with kindness, though, just as this book is written to gently guide you along in your journey to become a happy gardener.

Just one more thing. No one gardens alone. You included! So, pass along your gardening knowledge, and maybe this book, to someone you know. After all, that's how gardeners do it, passing along one plant to another, one tip to another, one encouragement to another so that everyone has a chance to live their best gardening life.

Thank you, and happy gardening now and forever.

ACKNOWLEDGMENTS

Publishing a book is never a solo endeavor. Many thanks to my sister, Sherry Weir, who read early versions of the chapters in this book and provided feedback. Also, thank you to my nephew, Ty Hayden, who designed the cover. Even more thanks to Deb Wiley, who provided content and copy editing. Thank you also to readers of my previous books for their kind words that inspired me to write this book of essays. I hope they, along with new readers, find both wisdom and humor in these pages that will enrich their gardening lives the way good compost improves a garden.

All errors are mine!

ABOUT THE AUTHOR

Carol J. Michel is an award-winning author focusing on gardening humor with occasional forays into children's books. As the holder of degrees in both horticulture and computer technology, she spent over three decades making a living in healthcare IT while making a life in her garden. She is also the keeper of the world's largest hoe collection, and her library is a sanctuary for old gardening books. She currently gardens in Indiana, at a place she calls May Dreams Gardens.

For more information, visit www.caroljmichel.com.

ALSO BY CAROL J. MICHEL

For gardeners, because humor does help a garden grow:

Potted and Pruned: Living a Gardening Life

Homegrown and Handpicked: A Year in a Gardening Life

Seeded and Sodded: Thoughts from a Gardening Life

Creatures and Critters: Who's in My Garden

And for children:

The Christmas Cottontail: A Story for Gardeners of All Ages